**W9-CFK-761**

Watch It Grow

# Silkworms

by Martha E. H. Rustad

**Consulting editor:** Gail Saunders-Smith, PhD

**Consultant:** Laura Jesse
Plant and Insect Diagnostic Clinic
Iowa State University, Ames, Iowa

Capstone
press

Mankato, Minnesota

Pebble Books are published by Capstone Press,
151 Good Counsel Drive, P.O. Box 669, Mankato, Minnesota 56002.
www.capstonepress.com

1 2 3 4 5 6 14 13 12 11 10 09

*Library of Congress Cataloging-in-Publication Data*
Rustad, Martha E. H. (Martha Elizabeth Hillman), 1975–
  Silkworms / by Martha E. H. Rustad.
  p. cm. — (Pebble books. Watch it grow)
  Includes bibliographical references and index.
  Summary: "Simple text and photographs present the life cycle of the silkworm
moth" — Provided by publisher.
    ISBN-13: 978-1-4296-2230-1 (hardcover)   ISBN-10: 1-4296-2230-X (hardcover)
    ISBN-13: 978-1-4296-3447-2 (softcover)     ISBN-10: 1-4296-3447-2 (softcover)
    1. Silkworms — Life cycles — Juvenile literature. I. Title.
QL561.B6R87 2009
595.78 — dc22                                                    2008026944

# Note to Parents and Teachers

The Watch It Grow set supports national science standards related
to life science. This book describes and illustrates silkworms.
The images support early readers in understanding the text. The
repetition of words and phrases helps early readers learn new
words. This book also introduces early readers to subject-specific
vocabulary words, which are defined in the Glossary section. Early
readers may need assistance to read some words and to use the
Table of Contents, Glossary, Read More, Internet Sites, and Index
sections of the book.

# Table of Contents

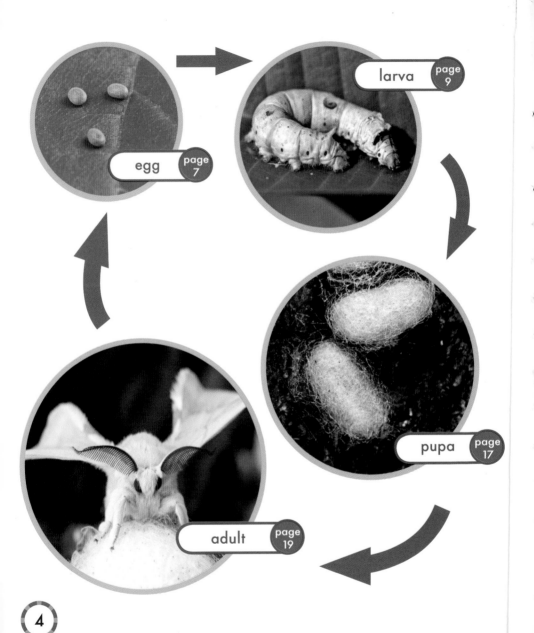

egg *page 7*

larva *page 9*

pupa *page 17*

adult *page 19*

## Metamorphosis

Silkworm moths are
hairy insects.
These insects go through
metamorphosis as they grow.

eggs

## From Egg to Larva

Silkworm moths begin life as tiny eggs. A female moth lays as many as 500 eggs in the fall.

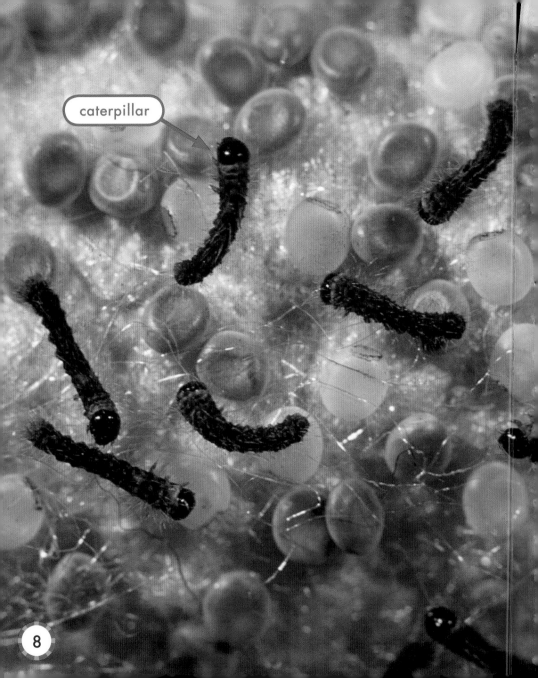

caterpillar

Silkworm caterpillars hatch
from eggs in spring.
They are black and hairy.
The caterpillars are
also called larvae.

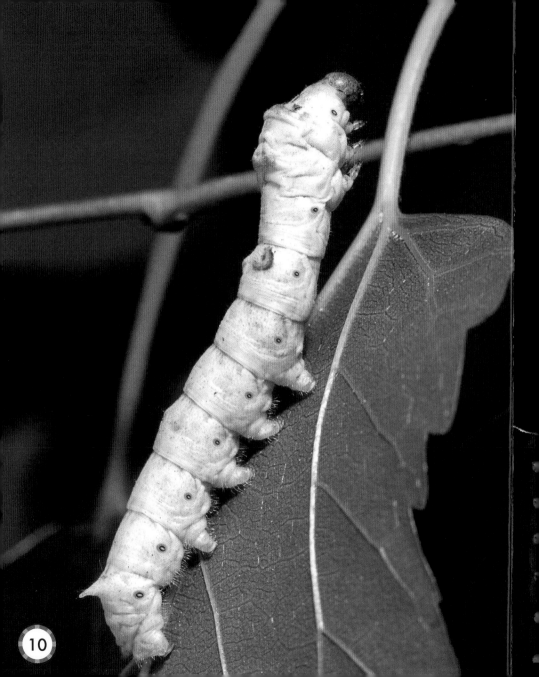

Silkworm larvae molt
four times as they grow.
Their skin is
smooth and white
after their first molt.

Silkworm larvae eat
only mulberry leaves.
They eat and grow quickly.

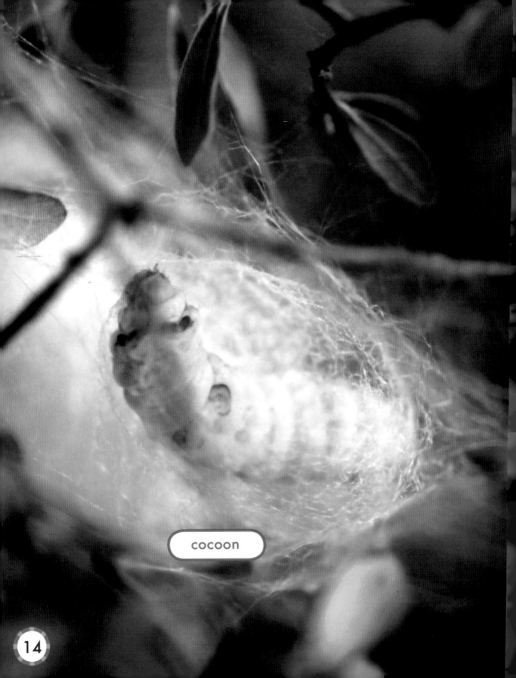

cocoon

# From Pupa to Adult

Larvae spin cocoons
about a month after hatching.
Each cocoon is
one long silk thread.

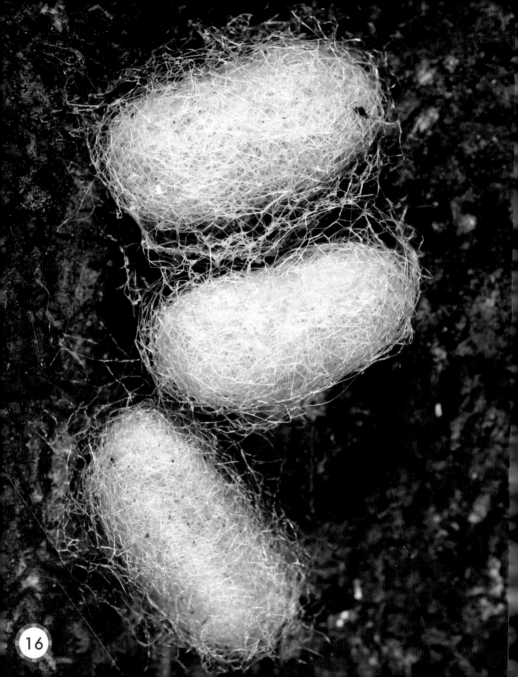

In the cocoon,
the silkworm is a pupa.
It grows adult body parts.
The pupa is an adult
in about three weeks.

The adult sprays a liquid
on the cocoon from inside.
The liquid makes a small hole.
The adult silkworm moth
crawls out of the cocoon.

Adult silkworm moths have big bodies and small wings. They cannot fly. Instead, they walk on their six legs.

# Glossary

**cocoon** — a covering made of silky thread; insects make a cocoon to protect themselves while they change from larvae to pupae.

**hatch** — to break out of an egg

**insect** — a small animal with a hard outer shell, six legs, three body sections, and two antennae; most insects have wings.

**larva** — an insect at the stage between egg and pupa; the plural of larva is larvae.

**metamorphosis** — the series of changes some animals go through as they develop from eggs to adults

**molt** — to shed skin or an outer shell so a new covering can be seen; when this process happens once, it is also called a molt.

**pupa** — an insect at the stage between a larva and an adult; the plural of pupa is pupae.

# Read More

**Jacobs, Liza.** *Silkworms.* Wild, Wild World. San Diego: Blackbirch Press, 2003.

**Macken, JoAnn Early.** *The Life Cycle of a Moth.* Things with Wings. Milwaukee, Wis.: Weekly Reader Early Learning Library, 2006.

# Internet Sites

FactHound offers a safe, fun way to find educator-approved Internet sites related to this book.

Here's what you do:

1. Visit *www.facthound.com*
2. Choose your grade level.
3. Begin your search.

This book's ID number is 9781429622301.

FactHound will fetch the best sites for you!

# Index

**Word Count: 160**
**Grade: 1**
**Early-Intervention Level: 17**

**Editorial Credits**
Erika L. Shores, editor; Alison Thiele, designer; Marcie Spence, photo researcher

**Photo Credits**
Bruce Coleman Inc./Wardene Weisser, 6
Capstone Press/Karon Dubke, 4 (eggs), 6 (eggs)
Cenap Refik ONGAN/123RF, cover (cocoon), 14
Dwight R. Kuhn, 8, 10, 18
iStockphoto/BMPix, 1; HotDuck2, 4 (cocoons), 16; JGPhotography,
        cover (caterpillar), 4 (caterpillar); iStockphoto/VickieSichau,
        cover (moth), 4 (moth), 20
Shutterstock/zhuda, 12